♥: _____ & ♥: _____

WE BEGAN RECORDING OUR YEAR TOGETHER ON:

WE COMPLETED FILLING OUT OUR YEAR TOGETHER ON:

WHAT A GRAND THING,
to be loved!
WHAT A GRANDER THING
still, to love!

—VICTOR HUGO

a Year with You

A KEEPSAKE JOURNAL FOR TWO TO SHARE

sourcebooks

Copyright © 2016 Sourcebooks, Inc.
Cover and internal design © 2016 by Sourcebooks, Inc.
Cover design by Sourcebooks, Inc.
Cover images/illustrations © saknakorn/Getty Images, David Malan/Getty Images

Sourcebooks and the colophon are registered trademarks of Sourcebooks, Inc.

Published by Sourcebooks, Inc.
P.O. Box 4410, Naperville, Illinois 60567–4410
(630) 961–3900
FAX: (630) 961–2168
www.sourcebooks.com

Printed and bound in China.
LEO 10 9 8 7 6 5 4 3

INTRODUCTION

No two people are alike, and no two relationships follow the same path. Who best to write your love story but you? Map your relationship and create a time capsule of who you were and who you're becoming over the span of a year. Designed in a unique daily interactive format for two, this journal is intended to be self-reflective; to record your milestones, thoughts, feelings and tender moments; and help bond, deepen, and record your relationship. *A Year with You* is a fun adventure for new relationships, AND relationships that have stood the test of time. The 365 prompts, with tear-out love notes on every page, make it easy to journal together and add volumes to your story year after year.

day 1

MY RESOLUTION FOR US THIS YEAR IS...

♥ : _____

_____

_____

♥ : _____

_____

_____

day 2

IN ONE YEAR I HOPE WE ARE...

♥ : _____

♥ : _____

Love doesn't make the world go 'round. Love is what makes the ride worthwhile.

—FRANKLIN P. JONES

♡

day 3

THE HOPE I HAVE FOR THIS YEAR IS...

♥ : _____

_____

_____

♥ : _____

_____

_____

day 4

THE FEAR I HOPE TO CONQUER THIS YEAR IS...

♥ : _____

♥ : _____

day **5**

IF I HAD TO DESCRIBE YOU TO SOMEONE WHO
HAS NEVER MET YOU, I WOULD SAY...

♥ :

♥ :

day **6**

THIS YEAR I'M READY TO LET GO OF...

♥ :

♥ :

OF COURSE I LIKE YOU, you're you!
♡

day 7

YOU INSPIRE ME TO...

♥ :

♥ :

day 8

TODAY I AM GRATEFUL FOR...

♥ :

♥ :

day **9**

WHAT I REMEMBER ABOUT THE DAY I MET YOU IS...

♥ :
_____

_____

♥ :
_____

_____

day **10**

IF I COULD BOTTLE ONE FEELING IT WOULD BE...

♥ :
_____

♥ :
_____

IN A SEA OF PEOPLE, my eyes will always search FOR YOURS. ♡

day 11

MY FAVORITE INSIDE JOKE WE SHARE IS...

♥ : _____

_____

_____

♥ : _____

_____

_____

day 12

HAVE YOU EVER NOTICED...?

♥ : _____

♥ : _____

day 13

THE THING I LOVE MOST ABOUT "US" IS...

♥ : _____

_____

_____

♥ : _____

_____

_____

day 14

MY GUILTY PLEASURE IS...

♥ : _____

♥ : _____

ANYONE CAN BE PASSIONATE, BUT IT TAKES **real lovers to be silly.**
—ROSE FRANKEN ♡

day 15

THE MOST ROMANTIC THING YOU'VE EVER DONE IS...

♥ : _____

_____

_____

♥ : _____

_____

_____

day 16

THE MOST LOVING THING YOU'VE EVER DONE IS...

♥ : _____

♥ : _____

day **17**

IF I COULD BOTTLE ONE MEMORY AND RELEASE IT
ONCE IN A WHILE TO RELIVE IT, IT WOULD BE...

♥ :

♥ :

day **18**

LOVE TO ME IS...

♥ :

_____

♥ :

_____

When I saw you I fell in love,
and you smiled because you knew.

—ARRIGO BOITO

♡

day 19

IF TIME TRAVEL WERE AN OPTION, I'D LIKE TO GO...
(PLACE AND TIME)

♥ :

♥ :

day 20

I WOULD TAKE . . . ON MY TIME-TRAVELING ADVENTURE.

♥ : _____

♥ : _____

day 21

I APPRECIATE IT WHEN YOU...

♥ :
_____

_____

♥ :
_____

_____

_____

day 22

IT IRKS ME WHEN YOU...

♥ :
_____

♥ :
_____

Two people in love,
alone, isolated from the world,
that's very beautiful.
—MILAN KUNDERA, IDENTITY

♡

day 23

PEOPLE SAY, "I'D DO ANYTHING FOR YOU."
I DRAW THE LINE AT...

♥ :

♥ :

day 24

MY ACHILLES HEEL IS...

♥ : _____

♥ : _____

day 25

LET'S DO SOMETHING SILLY TOGETHER. I HAVE A FEW IDEAS...

♥ : _____

_____

_____

♥ : _____

_____

_____

day 26

I'D NEVER... WITH ANYONE BUT YOU.

♥ : _____

♥ : _____

Love is or it ain't.
THIN LOVE AIN'T LOVE AT ALL.
—TONI MORRISON, *BELOVED* ♥

day 27

I'VE NEVER ADMITTED THIS TO ANYONE BUT I ONCE...

♥ : _____

_____

_____

♥ : _____

_____

_____

day 28

THE SMELL OF . . . IS SOOTHING.

♥ : _____

♥ : _____

day 29

MY INNER THREE-YEAR-OLD LIKES...

♥ : _____

_____

_____

♥ : _____

_____

_____

day 30

A YEAR FROM TODAY I'D LIKE TO FEEL...

♥ : _____

♥ : _____

Being silly with you
MAKES ME FORGET ANY HARD DAY.

♡

day 31

THE MOST INTERESTING PERSON I'VE MET
IN THE LAST SIX MONTHS IS...

♥ :

♥ :

day 32

I WISH I WERE A LITTLE MORE...

♥ :

♥ :

day 33

IF I COULD MAKE UP MY OWN HOLIDAY IT WOULD BE CALLED . . . AND IT WOULD BE A CELEBRATION OF...

♥ :

_____

_____

♥ :

_____

_____

day 34

I WISH I WERE A LITTLE LESS...

♥ :

_____

♥ :

_____

HE'S MORE MYSELF THAN I AM. WHATEVER OUR SOULS ARE MADE OF, HIS AND MINE ARE THE SAME.

—EMILY BRONTË, WUTHERING HEIGHTS

♡

day 35

THE BEST THREE THINGS I'VE EVER DONE ARE...

♥ : _____

_____

_____

♥ : _____

_____

_____

day 36

I WISH YOU WERE A LITTLE LESS...

♥ : _____

♥ : _____

day 37

THE TOP THREE THINGS ON MY BUCKET LIST ARE...

♥ : _____

_____

♥ : _____

_____

_____

day 38

I WISH YOU WERE A LITTLE MORE...

♥ : _____

♥ : _____

IF YOU LOVED SOMEONE, YOU LOVED HIM, AND WHEN YOU HAD NOTHING ELSE TO GIVE, YOU STILL GAVE HIM LOVE.

—GEORGE ORWELL, 1984

♡

day 39

THE TOP THREE THINGS ON OUR BUCKET LIST ARE:

♥ : _____

_____

♥ : _____

_____

day 40

THE BEST THREE THINGS WE'VE DONE TOGETHER ARE...

♥ : _____

_____

♥ : _____

_____

day 41

I'D LIKE TO CHANGE . . . BECAUSE IT BOTHERS YOU.

♥ : _____

_____

♥ : _____

_____

day 42

THE LAST TIME YOU MADE ME LAUGH OUT LOUD WAS...

♥ : _____

_____

♥ : _____

_____

THERE IS NO REMEDY FOR LOVE, but to love more.

—HENRY DAVID THOREAU

day 43

NAME THREE THINGS IT WOULD BE HARD TO LIVE WITHOUT...

♥ :

♥ :

day 44

I LOVE IT WHEN WE...

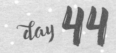

♥ : _____

♥ : _____

day **45**

NAME THREE THINGS THAT ARE OVERRATED:

♥ :
_____

_____

♥ :
_____

_____

day **46**

I CAN'T WAIT UNTIL WE...

♥ :
_____

♥ :
_____

Real love stories never have endings.

—RICHARD BACH ♡

day 47

AS A CHILD, I WAS...

♥ : _____

_____

_____

♥ : _____

_____

_____

day 48

CHANGE IS...

♥ : _____

♥ : _____

day **49**

THE MOST REWARDING CHANGE FOR ME WAS...

♥ : _____

_____

_____

♥ : _____

_____

_____

day **50**

WHEN I WAS YOUNGER I IMAGINED MY PARTNER TO BE...

♥ : _____

♥ : _____

WELL THE FUTURE FOR ME IS ALREADY A THING OF THE PAST
YOU WERE MY FIRST LOVE AND YOU WILL BE MY LAST.

— BOB DYLAN

♡

day **51**

YOU REMIND ME TO BE...

♥ : _____

_____

_____

♥ : _____

_____

_____

day **52**

I AM THANKFUL THAT YOUR FAMILY THINKS ME TO BE...

♥ : _____

♥ : _____

day 53

I LIKE DOING . . . FOR YOU BECAUSE IT MAKES YOU HAPPY.

♥ :

♥ :

day 54

I HATE THAT . . . MAKES YOU SAD.

♥ : _____

♥ : _____

You pierce my soul.
I AM HALF AGONY, HALF HOPE...
I HAVE LOVED NONE BUT YOU.

—JANE AUSTEN, *PERSUASION*

♡

day **55**

IF I COULD CHOOSE BETWEEN KNOWING THE
FUTURE OR ALTERING THE PAST, I WOULD PICK...

♥ :

♥ :

day **56**

WHY DON'T YOU EVER...?

♥ :

♥ :

day 57

THREE THINGS I'M GRATEFUL FOR TODAY ARE...

♥ : _____

_____

_____

♥ : _____

_____

_____

day 58

IF THERE WERE NO CONSEQUENCES, I WOULD...

♥ : _____

♥ : _____

HE WHO LOVES, FLIES, RUNS, AND REJOICES; he is free and nothing HOLDS HIM BACK.

—HENRI MATISSE

♡

day 59

IF I WERE A SUPERHERO, MY SUPERPOWER WOULD BE...

♥ : _____

_____

_____

♥ : _____

_____

_____

day 60

AND MY NAME WOULD BE...

♥ : _____

♥ : _____

day **61**

IF YOU WERE MY SIDEKICK, YOUR
SUPERPOWER WOULD BE...

♥ :
_____

_____

_____

♥ :
_____

_____

_____

day **62**

AND YOUR NAME WOULD BE...

♥ :
_____

♥ :
_____

Love is an irresistible desire
to be irresistibly desired.

—ROBERT FROST

♡

day **63**

I'VE ALWAYS WONDERED WHY...

♥ :

♥ :

day **64**

TRUTH OR DARE?

♥ :

_____

♥ :

_____

day 65

...MAKES ME PANIC.

♥:
_____
_____
_____
♥:
_____
_____
_____

day 66

...CALMS ME DOWN.

♥:
_____
♥:
_____

Do I love you? My God,
if your love were a grain of sand,
mine would be a universe of beaches.

—WILLIAM GOLDMAN, THE PRINCESS BRIDE

♡

day **67**

I'D LIKE TO GO BACK IN TIME TO WHEN WE...

♥ : _____

_____

♥ : _____

_____

day **68**

IF I COULD MAKE A CHANGE TO THE DAY WE MET, IT WOULD BE...

♥ : _____

_____

♥ : _____

_____

day 69

YOU ARE NOT...

♥ : _____

_____

♥ : _____

_____

day 70

I AM NOT...

♥ : _____

_____

♥ : _____

_____

LOVE IS NOT AFFECTIONATE FEELING, BUT A STEADY WISH FOR THE LOVED PERSON'S ULTIMATE GOOD AS FAR AS IT CAN BE OBTAINED.

—C.S. LEWIS

day 71

THE CUTEST THING YOU DID THIS WEEK WAS...

♥ : _____

_____

_____

♥ : _____

_____

_____

day 72

I LIKE IT WHEN YOU...

♥ : _____

♥ : _____

day 73

...IS MISSING IN MY LIFE.

♥ :

♥ :

day 74

I COULD LIVE WITHOUT... IN MY LIFE.

♥ :

♥ :

day 75

THE NEW THING I'M OBSESSED WITH THESE DAYS IS...

♥ : _____

_____

_____

♥ : _____

_____

_____

day 76

I'M OVER...

♥ : _____

♥ : _____

day 77

...FEELS UNFINISHED.

♥ : _____

_____

♥ : _____

_____

_____

day 78

I'M HAPPY WITH...

♥ : _____

♥ : _____

ONCE UPON A TIME THERE WAS A BOY WHO LOVED A GIRL, AND HER LAUGHTER WAS A QUESTION HE WANTED TO SPEND HIS WHOLE LIFE ANSWERING.

—NICOLE KRAUSS, THE HISTORY OF LOVE

♡

day 79

IF I COULD ENFORCE A WORLDWIDE RULE, IT WOULD BE...
(IN ADDITION TO WORLD PEACE)

♥ :

♥ :

day 80

IF I COULD GET RID OF ONE THING FOREVER, IT WOULD BE...

♥ : _____

♥ : _____

day 81

IF I COULD PLAN A ROMANTIC GETAWAY FOR US, WE WOULD...

♥ :

_____

_____

♥ :

_____

_____

day 82

THE LAST TRIP WE TOOK TOGETHER WAS...

♥ :

_____

♥ :

_____

My happy place is wherever we are together. ♡

day 83

SOME THINGS I CHECKED OFF MY TO-DO LIST ARE...

♥ : _____

_____

_____

♥ : _____

_____

_____

day 84

THE NUMBER ONE THING I'D STILL LIKE TO CHECK OFF IS...

♥ : _____

♥ : _____

day 85

TODAY I AM THANKFUL FOR...

♥ : _____

_____

♥ : _____

_____

day 86

IN THE GRAND SCHEME OF THINGS . . . IS SO SMALL.

♥ : _____

♥ : _____

The best thing to hold onto in life is each other.

— AUDREY HEPBURN

♡

day **87**

MY FAVORITE HOLIDAY IS...

♥ : _____

♥ : _____

day **88**

MY FAVORITE HOLIDAY TRADITION IS...

♥ : _____
_____
_____

♥ : _____
_____
_____

day **89**

I MISS...

♥ :

♥ :

day **90**

...REMINDS ME THAT I'M IN LOVE.

♥ :

♥ :

Morning without you is
a dwindled dawn.

—EMILY DICKINSON

♡

day **91**

IF I COULD HAVE LUNCH WITH ANYONE IN THE
WORLD (BESIDES YOU), I WOULD PICK...

♥:

♥:

day **92**

IF I COULD CHOOSE ANY SPORT TO EXCEL AT, IT WOULD BE...

♥:
_____

♥:
_____

day 93

THE LAST DREAM I CAN REMEMBER IS...

♥ :
_____

_____

♥ :
_____

_____

day 94

IF I COULD CHOOSE ANY ART TO EXCEL AT, IT WOULD BE...

♥ :
_____

♥ :
_____

YOU KNOW YOU'RE IN LOVE WHEN YOU CAN'T FALL ASLEEP BECAUSE REALITY IS FINALLY BETTER THAN YOUR DREAMS.

—DR. SEUSS

♡

day 95

MY PLAYLIST FOR YOU INCLUDES THESE SONGS:

♥ : _____

_____

_____

♥ : _____

_____

_____

day 96

WHEN I'M WITH YOU, I FEEL LIKE...

♥ : _____

♥ : _____

day **97**

IF I COULD QUIT MY DAY JOB TO PURSUE MY PASSION, I WOULD...

♥ : _____

_____

_____

♥ : _____

_____

_____

day **98**

I'D LIKE TO LEARN HOW TO...

♥ : _____

♥ : _____

Love makes your soul
crawl out from its hiding place.
—ZORA NEALE HURSTON, *THEIR EYES WERE WATCHING GOD*

♡

day **99**

I DO MY BEST THINKING
AND GET MY BEST IDEAS WHEN I...

♥ :

♥ :

day **100**

IS IGNORANCE BLISS?

♥ : _____

♥ : _____

day **101**

MY FAVORITE NEW DISCOVERY IS...

♥ :
_____

_____

♥ :
_____

_____

_____

day **102**

I LEARNED . . . FROM YOU.

♥ :
_____

♥ :
_____

Love isn't something you find.

LOVE IS SOMETHING THAT FINDS YOU.

—LORETTA YOUNG

♡

day 103

I REGRET NOT FINISHING...

♥ : _____

_____

♥ : _____

_____

day 104

I'M GLAD I FINISHED...

♥ : _____

_____

♥ : _____

_____

day **105**

I WOULD HIRE YOU BECAUSE...

♥ : _____

_____

♥ : _____

_____

day **106**

I WOULD FIRE YOU BECAUSE...

♥ : _____

_____

♥ : _____

_____

WITH HIM, LIFE WAS ROUTINE;
WITHOUT HIM, LIFE WAS UNBEARABLE.

—HARPER LEE, TO KILL A MOCKINGBIRD

♡

day **107**

I'D LOVE TO GET RID OF...

♥ : _____

_____

_____

♥ : _____

_____

_____

day **108**

I BET YOU WOULD BE BETTER AT . . . THAN I AM.

♥ : _____

♥ : _____

day 109

MY LOVE LANGUAGE IS...

♥ :

♥ :

day 110

I WANT ... MORE THAN ANYTHING.

♥ : _____

♥ : _____

I DON'T WANT NORMAL, AND EASY, AND SIMPLE.
I WANT PAINFUL, DIFFICULT, DEVASTATING,
LIFE-CHANGING, EXTRAORDINARY LOVE.

—KERRY WASHINGTON AS OLIVIA POPE, SCANDAL

♡

day 111

MY FAVORITE TV SHOW RIGHT NOW IS...

♥: _____

_____

_____

♥: _____

_____

_____

day 112

MY FAVORITE RESTAURANT RIGHT NOW IS...

♥: _____

♥: _____

day 113

YOU AND I ARE PARTNERS BECAUSE...

♥ : _____

_____

♥ : _____

_____

day 114

MY MEMOIR WILL BE TITLED...

♥ : _____

♥ : _____

WHEN YOU LOVE SOMEONE, YOU LOVE THE PERSON AS THEY ARE, AND NOT AS YOU'D LIKE THEM TO BE.

—LEO TOLSTOY

♡

day **115**

I DON'T . . . ENOUGH.

♥ :

♥ :

day **116**

THE COUPLE I MOST ADMIRE IS...

♥ :

♥ :

day 117

I THINK WE'RE HERE TO...

♥ : _____

_____

_____

♥ : _____

_____

_____

day 118

IF WE HAD NEVER MET, I NEVER WOULD HAVE LEARNED TO...

♥ : _____

♥ : _____

You can, you should, and if you're brave enough to start, you will.

—STEPHEN KING, ON WRITING: A MEMOIR OF THE CRAFT

♡

day 119

IF I HAD AN EXTRA TEN DOLLARS IN MY POCKET, I WOULD...

♥ : _____

_____

♥ : _____

_____

day 120

THE PERSON THAT ALWAYS TELLS IT TO ME STRAIGHT IS...

♥ : _____

♥ : _____

day 121

IF I CAME INTO AN UNEXPECTED INHERITANCE, I WOULD...

♥ : _____

_____

_____

♥ : _____

_____

_____

day 122

OUR LOVE STORY WOULD BE TITLED...

♥ : _____

♥ : _____

THERE ARE ALL KINDS OF LOVE IN THE WORLD, but never the same love twice.

— F. SCOTT FITZGERALD, "THE SENSIBLE THING"

♡

day **123**

I HOPE I NEVER...

♥ : _____

_____

♥ : _____

_____

day **124**

I KNOW I CAN ALWAYS COUNT ON YOU TO...

♥ : _____

_____

♥ : _____

_____

day **125**

YOU ARE MY...

♥ : _____

_____

♥ : _____

_____

day **126**

WHEN WE GROW OLD, I IMAGINE US TO BE...

♥ : _____

_____

♥ : _____

_____

day 127

I IMAGINE HEAVEN TO BE...

♥ : _____

_____

_____

♥ : _____

_____

_____

day 128

I DON'T BELIEVE IN...

♥ : _____

♥ : _____

day **129**

WHEN I NEED A GOOD LAUGH, I THINK OF...

♥ : _____

_____

♥ : _____

_____

day **130**

...ALWAYS MAKES ME SAD.

♥ : _____

♥ : _____

LOVE AT FIRST SIGHT IS EASY TO UNDERSTAND; IT'S WHEN TWO PEOPLE HAVE BEEN LOOKING AT EACH OTHER FOR A LIFETIME THAT IT BECOMES A MIRACLE.

—SAM LEVENSON

♡

day **131**

SOMETHING I'VE LEARNED ABOUT
MYSELF THIS YEAR IS THAT I...

♥ :

♥ :

day **132**

SOMETHING I'VE LEARNED ABOUT YOU THIS YEAR IS THAT YOU...

♥ :

_____

♥ :

_____

day 133

WHAT MAKES YOU GET UP IN THE MORNING?

♥ : _____

_____

_____

♥ : _____

_____

_____

day 134

...MAKES THE WORLD GO ROUND.

♥ : _____

♥ : _____

Kissing—AND I MEAN LIKE, YUMMY, SMACKING KISSING—IS THE MOST DELICIOUS, MOST BEAUTIFUL AND PASSIONATE THING THAT TWO PEOPLE CAN DO, BAR NONE. BETTER THAN SEX, HANDS DOWN.

—DREW BARRYMORE ♡

day **135**

THE SECRET TO HAPPINESS IS...

♥ :
_____

_____

_____

♥ :
_____

_____

_____

day **136**

SEEK AND YOU SHALL FIND...

♥ :
_____

♥ :
_____

day 137

LET'S . . . TOGETHER.

♥ : _____

_____

♥ : _____

_____

_____

day 138

I LIKE DOING . . . ALONE.

♥ : _____

♥ : _____

Every day I find new things to love about you. ♡

day **139**

THE FIRST THINGS THAT COME TO MIND WHEN I HEAR THE WORDS...

CAKE: _____   _____

HOT: _____   _____

DROP: _____   _____

JOURNAL: _____   _____

SHEETS: _____   _____

DIRTY: _____   _____

day **140**

MY FAVORITE PICTURE OF THE TWO OF US IS...

♥ : _____

♥ : _____

day 141

I DON'T TELL YOU ENOUGH THAT...

♥ : _____

_____

♥ : _____

_____

day 142

THE BEST COMPLIMENT YOU'VE GIVEN ME WAS...

♥ : _____

♥ : _____

LOVE HER, LOVE HER, LOVE HER! IF SHE FAVORS YOU, LOVE HER. IF SHE WOUNDS YOU, LOVE HER. IF SHE TEARS YOUR HEART TO PIECES—AND AS IT GETS OLDER AND STRONGER, IT WILL TEAR DEEPER—LOVE HER, LOVE HER, LOVE HER!

—CHARLES DICKENS, <u>GREAT EXPECTATIONS</u>

day **143**

TODAY I WISH I WOULD HAVE...

♥ : _____

_____

_____

♥ : _____

_____

_____

_____

day **144**

MY NEW FAVORITE DESSERT IS...

♥ : _____

♥ : _____

day **145**

TODAY I WISH I DIDN'T...

♥: _____

_____

_____

♥: _____

_____

_____

day **146**

MY NEW FAVORITE DRINK IS...

♥: _____

♥: _____

Love me when I least deserve it,
BECAUSE THAT'S WHEN I REALLY NEED IT.
—SWEDISH PROVERB

♡

day **147**

A NEW PLACE I'D LIKE TO TRY IS...

♥ : _____

_____

_____

♥ : _____

_____

_____

day **148**

IF MONEY OR TIME WEREN'T AN ISSUE I WOULD BOOK US A TRIP TO...

♥ : _____

♥ : _____

day **149**

SOMETIMES I WISH WE COULD TRADE
PLACES SO THAT I COULD...

♥ :

♥ :

day **150**

TODAY I DAYDREAMED ABOUT...

♥ :

♥ :

Come, live in my heart and pay no rent.

—SAMUEL LOVER

♡

day **151**

I THINK WE WERE PUT HERE BECAUSE...

♥: _____

_____

_____

♥: _____

_____

_____

_____

day **152**

HAVE YOU EVER WONDERED WHY...

♥: _____

♥: _____

day 153

I'VE NEVER TOLD ANYONE THAT...

♥ : _____

_____

_____

♥ : _____

_____

_____

day 154

I SOMETIMES LIE ABOUT...

♥ : _____

♥ : _____

There is no love without friendship.
THANKS FOR BEING MY FRIEND!

♡

day **155**

TRUTH OR DARE?

♥ :

♥ :

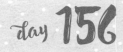

day **156**

IF I COULD CHANGE MY NAME, I WOULD CHANGE IT TO...

♥ : _____

♥ : _____

day 157

NEVER DISCUSS . . . ON AN EMPTY STOMACH.

♥ :

♥ :

day 158

IT IS RUDE TO . . . IN PUBLIC.

♥ :

♥ :

day **159**

I'M OLD-FASHIONED WHEN IT COMES TO...

♥: _____

_____

♥: _____

_____

day **160**

I'M PROGRESSIVE WHEN IT COMES TO...

♥: _____

_____

♥: _____

_____

day 161

YOU BRING OUT THE . . . IN ME.

♥ : _____

_____

♥ : _____

_____

day 162

I HOPE I BRING OUT THE . . . IN YOU.

♥ : _____

_____

♥ : _____

_____

I LOVE YOU NOT ONLY FOR WHAT YOU ARE,
BUT FOR WHAT I AM WHEN I AM WITH YOU.

—ROY CROFT, "LOVE"

♡

day **163**

I'M EMBARRASSED TO ADMIT I LIKE...

♥ : _____

_____

_____

♥ : _____

_____

_____

day **164**

I'M EMBARRASSED TO ADMIT <u>YOU</u> LIKE...

♥ : _____

♥ : _____

day **165**

I WOULD NEVER TRADE... FOR ANYTHING.

♥ :

♥ :

day **166**

BEST BOOK I'VE EVER READ:

♥ :
_____

♥ :
_____

WE WERE TOGETHER—ALL ELSE HAS LONG
BEEN FORGOTTEN BY ME.

—WALT WHITMAN, "ONCE I PASS'D THROUGH A POPULOUS CITY"

♡

day 167

THE LAST MOVIE THAT MADE ME CRY WAS...

♥ : _____

_____

_____

♥ : _____

_____

_____

day 168

THE LAST NEWS STORY THAT MADE ME CRY WAS...

♥ : _____

♥ : _____

day **169**

OUR FUTURE FEELS...

♥ : _____

_____

_____

♥ : _____

_____

_____

day **170**

OUR PAST REMINDS ME...

♥ : _____

♥ : _____

Grow old with me!
The best is yet to be.

— ROBERT BROWNING, "RABBI BEN EZRA"

♡

day 171

WHEN I LOOK BACK ON THIS YEAR, I WANT TO REMEMBER...

♥ : _____

_____

_____

♥ : _____

_____

_____

day 172

THE LAST BOOK THAT MADE AN IMPACT ON ME WAS...

♥ : _____

♥ : _____

day **173**

WHEN I LOOK BACK ON TODAY, I WANT TO REMEMBER...

♥ : _____

_____

_____

♥ : _____

_____

_____

day **174**

THE LAST SHOW THAT MADE AN IMPACT ON ME WAS...

♥ : _____

♥ : _____

TO GET THE FULL value OF A JOY YOU must HAVE SOMEBODY TO DIVIDE IT WITH.

— MARK TWAIN

♡

day **175**

MY ALTER EGO'S NAME IS...

♥ : _____

♥ : _____

day **176**

(S)HE IS DIFFERENT FROM ME BECAUSE...

♥ : _____

_____

_____

♥ : _____

_____

_____

day 177

IF I COULD BE ANY TV CHARACTER, I WOULD BE...

♥:

♥:

day 178

IF I COULD BE ANY MOVIE CHARACTER, I WOULD BE...

♥:

_____

♥:

_____

AS HE READ, I fell in love THE WAY YOU FALL ASLEEP: SLOWLY, AND THEN ALL AT ONCE.

—JOHN GREEN, THE FAULT IN OUR STARS

♡

day **179**

IF I HAD CAPITAL AT MY DISPOSAL TO TURN ANY INVENTION INTO REALITY, I WOULD MAKE...

♥ :

♥ :

day **180**

FEAR IS...

♥ :

♥ :

day 181

NEXT YEAR AROUND THIS TIME I HOPE I AM...

♥ :

♥ :

day 182

NEXT YEAR AROUND THIS TIME I HOPE WE ARE...

♥ :

♥ :

IF I KNOW WHAT LOVE IS,
it is because of you.

—HERMANN HESSE, NARCISSUS AND GOLDMUND

♡

day 183

NEXT YEAR AROUND THIS TIME I HOPE I AM NOT...

♥ : _____

_____

_____

♥ : _____

_____

_____

day 184

NEXT YEAR AROUND THIS TIME I HOPE WE ARE NOT...

♥ : _____

♥ : _____

day **185**

THE THEME SONG FOR THIS WEEK IS...

♥ :

♥ :

day **186**

I LOVE IT WHEN YOU...

♥ :
_____

♥ :
_____

day 187

I'M FEELING OPTIMISTIC ABOUT...

♥ : _____

_____

_____

♥ : _____

_____

_____

day 188

I'M FEELING PESSIMISTIC ABOUT...

♥ : _____

♥ : _____

day **189**

...MAKES ME FEEL POWERFUL.

♥ : _____

_____

_____

♥ : _____

_____

_____

day **190**

...SCARES ME.

♥ : _____

♥ : _____

_____

IT TAKES COURAGE TO GROW UP AND
become who you really are.
—E.E. CUMMINGS

day **191**

MY FAVORITE QUOTE IS...

♥ :

♥ :

day **192**

I LOVE IT WHEN YOU TELL ME THE . . . STORY.

♥ :

♥ :

day **193**

A QUOTE I'D LIKE TO BE REMINDED OF SAYING IS...

♥ : _____

_____

_____

♥ : _____

_____

_____

day **194**

YOU ARE CUTE WHEN YOU...

♥ : _____

♥ : _____

The universe is made of stories, not of atoms.

—MURIEL RUKEYSER, "THE SPEED OF DARKNESS"

♡

day **195**

THE CLOSEST I'VE EVER GOTTEN TO A CELEBRITY WAS...

♥ : _____

_____

♥ : _____

_____

day **196**

MY CLOSEST CLAIM TO FAME WAS...

♥ : _____

_____

♥ : _____

_____

day 197

IT'S NEVER TOO LATE TO START
FRESH. I'D LIKE TO CHANGE...

♥ : _____

_____

♥ : _____

_____

day 198

I'M . . . WITH THE WAY THE YEAR IS UNFOLDING THUS FAR.

♥ : _____

_____

♥ : _____

_____

LOVE RECOGNIZES NO BARRIERS. IT JUMPS
HURDLES, LEAPS FENCES, PENETRATES WALLS TO
ARRIVE AT ITS DESTINATION FULL OF HOPE.

—MAYA ANGELOU

day **199**

WE COULD MAKE OUR RELATIONSHIP BETTER BY...

♥ : _____

_____

_____

♥ : _____

_____

_____

day **200**

I AM GLAD WE DID...

♥ : _____

♥ : _____

day 201

I LOVE . . . ABOUT US.

♥ : _____

_____

_____

♥ : _____

_____

_____

day 202

I'M GLAD WE DIDN'T...

♥ : _____

♥ : _____

IN VAIN HAVE I STRUGGLED. IT WILL NOT DO. MY FEELINGS WILL NOT BE REPRESSED. YOU MUST ALLOW ME TO TELL YOU HOW ARDENTLY I ADMIRE AND LOVE YOU.

—JANE AUSTEN, PRIDE AND PREJUDICE

♡

day **203**

TODAY WAS REWARDING BECAUSE...

♥ :

♥ :

day **204**

I APPRECIATE AND AM THANKFUL FOR...

♥ : _____

♥ : _____

day 205

I BET YOU DIDN'T KNOW THAT I...

♥ : _____

_____

_____

♥ : _____

_____

_____

day 206

I SECRETLY LOVE TO...

♥ : _____

♥ : _____

YOU ARE MY SUNSHINE. ♡

day **207**

...MAKES ME HAPPY.

♥ : _____

_____

♥ : _____

_____

day **208**

...ANNOYS ME SO MUCH.

♥ : _____

_____

♥ : _____

_____

day **209**

BEFORE I DRIFT TO SLEEP I THINK OF...

♥ : _____

_____

♥ : _____

_____

day **210**

MY FIRST THOUGHTS IN THE MORNING ARE ABOUT...

♥ : _____

_____

♥ : _____

_____

THE STORY OF LIFE IS QUICKER THAN THE WINK OF AN EYE, THE STORY OF LOVE IS HELLO AND GOODBYE. UNTIL WE MEET AGAIN.

—JIMI HENDRIX, "THE STORY OF LIFE"

♡

day **211**

WOULD YOU RATHER...

♥ : _____

_____

_____

♥ : _____

_____

_____

day **212**

WOULD YOU RATHER...

♥ : _____

♥ : _____

day **213**

MY FRIENDS WOULD DESCRIBE YOU AS...

♥ :

♥ :

day **214**

THE LAST TIME WE LAUGHED SO HARD IT HURT WAS...

♥ :

♥ :

The most wasted of all days
is one without laughter.

—E. E. CUMMINGS

♡

day 215

A PERFECT SATURDAY WITH YOU IS...

♥ : _____

_____

_____

♥ : _____

_____

_____

day 216

A PERFECT SATURDAY FOR "ME TIME" IS...

♥ : _____

♥ : _____

day 217

PARTNERSHIP IS...

♥ :

_____

_____

♥ :

_____

_____

day 218

THE MOST IMPORTANT INGREDIENTS IN A PARTNER ARE...

♥ :

_____

♥ :

_____

WE COME TO LOVE NOT BY FINDING A PERFECT PERSON, BUT BY LEARNING TO SEE AN IMPERFECT PERSON PERFECTLY.

—SAM KEEN

♡

day 219

THE MOST EXCITING MOMENT OF MY LIFE WAS...

♥ : _____

_____

_____

♥ : _____

_____

_____

day 220

I HOPE TO BECOME LESS . . . WITH TIME.

♥ : _____

♥ : _____

day 221

THE MOST EMBARRASSING MOMENT OF MY LIFE WAS...

♥: _____

_____

_____

♥: _____

_____

_____

day 222

I HOPE TO BECOME MORE . . . WITH TIME.

♥: _____

♥: _____

Love is the greatest refreshment in life.

—PABLO PICASSO ♡

day **223**

IN ORDER TO SPARE _____'S FEELINGS, I LIED ABOUT...

♥ : _____

_____

_____

♥ : _____

_____

_____

day **224**

SOMETHING YOU SHOULD ALWAYS LIE TO ME ABOUT IS...

♥ : _____

♥ : _____

day 225

IF I WERE TO PUT A MESSAGE IN A BOTTLE
FOR YOU, IT WOULD SAY...

♥ :

♥ :

day 226

IF I COULD ONLY SEND YOU A SINGLE WORD TO
SHOW YOU I CARE, THAT WORD WOULD BE...

♥ :

_____

♥ :

_____

HOW DO I LOVE THEE? LET ME COUNT THE
WAYS. I LOVE THEE TO THE DEPTH AND BREADTH
AND HEIGHT MY SOUL CAN REACH.

—ELIZABETH BARRETT BROWNING

♡

day **227**

THE FIRST THINGS THAT COME TO MIND WHEN I HEAR THE WORDS...

CHOCOLATE: _____ _____

SUN: _____ _____

LOVE: _____ _____

BLANKET: _____ _____

JOY: _____ _____

BUBBLE: _____ _____

day **228**

LET'S RUN AWAY TO...

♥ : _____

♥ : _____

day 229

THE SONG THAT BEST DESCRIBES HOW I GENERALLY FEEL ABOUT LIFE IS...

♥ : _____

_____

♥ : _____

_____

day 230

THE SONG THAT BEST DESCRIBES HOW I FEEL ABOUT YOU RIGHT NOW IS...

♥ : _____

_____

♥ : _____

_____

NO, WE'RE NOT PROMISED TOMORROW
So I'm gonna love you
LIKE I'M GONNA LOSE YOU.
LIKE I'M GONNA LOSE YOU"
—MEGHAN TRAINOR, "LIKE I'M GONNA LOSE YOU"
♡

day 231

BESIDES BEING A GREAT PARTNER TO ME, YOU ARE...

♥ : _____

_____

♥ : _____

_____

day 232

AN EXPERIENCE THAT HELPED US GROW TOGETHER WAS...

♥ : _____

_____

♥ : _____

_____

day 233

IF I COULD HAVE THREE WISHES GRANTED, THEY WOULD BE...

♥ : _____

_____

♥ : _____

_____

day 234

YOU HAVEN'T TRULY LIVED UNTIL YOU'VE...

♥ : _____

_____

♥ : _____

_____

The greatest thing you'll ever learn is to love and be loved in return.

— EDEN AHBEZ, "NATURE BOY"

♡

day 235

AN "AHA" MOMENT I'VE HAD ABOUT LIFE LATELY WAS...

♥ : _____

_____

_____

♥ : _____

_____

_____

day 236

AN "AHA" MOMENT I'VE HAD ABOUT US WAS...

♥ : _____

♥ : _____

day 237

IF I COULD FAST-FORWARD TIME TO GET TO A PLACE/
TIME I'M EXCITED ABOUT, I WOULD FAST-FORWARD TO...

♥ :

♥ :

day 238

IF I COULD CHOOSE BETWEEN BEING HAPPY AND
BEING INFLUENTIAL, I WOULD CHOOSE...

♥ :

♥ :

I'M LOOKING FOR LOVE. Real love.
RIDICULOUS, INCONVENIENT, CONSUMING,
CAN'T-LIVE-WITHOUT-EACH-OTHER LOVE.

—SARAH JESSICA PARKER AS CARRIE BRADSHAW, SEX AND THE CITY ♡

day 239

IF YOU LOVE SOMETHING...

♥ : _____

_____

♥ : _____

_____

day 240

IF YOU HATE SOMETHING...

♥ : _____

_____

♥ : _____

_____

day **241**

MY MOOD TODAY IS...

♥ : _____

_____

♥ : _____

_____

day **242**

BECAUSE...

♥ : _____

_____

♥ : _____

_____

We are most alive when we're in love.

—JOHN UPDIKE

♡

day **243**

MY FAVORITE SPOT IN THE WORLD IS...

♥ : _____

_____

_____

♥ : _____

_____

_____

day **244**

MY FAVORITE COMFORT FOOD IS...

♥ : _____

♥ : _____

day **245**

A LOVE LETTER FROM ME TO YOU:

♥ : _____

_____

_____

♥ : _____

_____

_____

day **246**

TODAY I'M HOPEFUL ABOUT...

♥ : _____

♥ : _____

AND THE SUNLIGHT CLASPS THE EARTH
AND THE MOONBEAMS KISS THE SEA—
WHAT ARE ALL THESE KISSINGS WORTH
IF THOU KISS NOT ME?

—PERCY BYSSHE SHELLEY, "LOVE'S PHILOSOPHY"

♡

day 247

THE FOOD I'M CURRENTLY OBSESSED WITH IS...

♥ : _____

_____

♥ : _____

_____

day 248

THE TV SHOW I'M CURRENTLY OBSESSED WITH IS...

♥ : _____

_____

♥ : _____

_____

day 249

IF I COULD GO BACK TO AN IMPORTANT FORK IN THE ROAD
AND MAKE A DIFFERENT DECISION, IT WOULD BE...

♥ :
_____

_____

_____

♥ :
_____

_____

_____

day 250

I LOVE . . . ABOUT YOU.

♥ :
_____

♥ :
_____

SEXINESS WEARS THIN AFTER A WHILE AND BEAUTY
FADES, BUT TO BE MARRIED TO A MAN WHO MAKES
YOU LAUGH EVERY DAY, AH, NOW THAT IS A TREAT.

—JOANNE WOODWARD

♡

day **251**

IF I COULD WRITE A NOTE TO MY TWENTY-
YEAR-OLD SELF, IT WOULD SAY...

♥ :

♥ :

day **252**

ONE LINE FROM A SONG THAT REMINDS ME OF YOU IS:

♥ :

_____

♥ :

_____

day **253**

IF I COULD WRITE A NOTE TO MY SEVENTY-
YEAR-OLD SELF, IT WOULD SAY...

♥ :
_____
_____
_____
♥ :
_____
_____

day **254**

...IS MY HERO.

♥ :
_____
♥ :
_____

i carry your heart with me
(i carry it in my heart)
—e.e. cummings ♡

day 255

THE SONG I AM CURRENTLY OBSESSED WITH IS...

♥ : _____

_____

♥ : _____

_____

day 256

MY FAVORITE MOVIE RIGHT NOW IS...

♥ : _____

_____

♥ : _____

_____

day **257**

I IMAGINE THE YEAR 2030 TO LOOK LIKE...

♥ : _____

_____

♥ : _____

_____

_____

day **258**

A HEADLINE FROM MY IMAGINED YEAR 2030 WOULD BE:

♥ : _____

♥ : _____

THERE YOU WERE AND THERE I WAS

Was it fate from above?

EITHER WAY I FOUND JUST WHAT I NEED.

—JOY WILLIAMS, "WHAT CAN I DO (BUT LOVE YOU)"

♡

day **259**

I HAVE NEVER...

♥ :
_____

_____

♥ :
_____

_____

day **260**

I WILL NEVER...

♥ :
_____

_____

♥ :
_____

_____

day 261

I MIGHT... BUT ONLY IF...

♥ :
_____

_____

♥ :
_____

_____

day 262

I WOULD DEFINITELY... IF...

♥ :
_____

_____

♥ :
_____

_____

We love because it's the only true adventure.

—NIKKI GIOVANNI ♡

day **263**

IF I COULD CHOOSE BETWEEN BEING OMNIPRESENT AND OMNISCIENT, I WOULD PICK...

♥ : _____

_____

♥ : _____

_____

day **264**

LIFE IS WORTH LIVING BECAUSE...

♥ : _____

_____

♥ : _____

_____

day 265

THE BRAVEST THING I THINK I'VE EVER DONE IS...

♥ : _____

_____

♥ : _____

_____

day 266

THE BRAVEST THING I THINK <u>YOU'VE</u> EVER DONE IS...

♥ : _____

_____

♥ : _____

_____

I have no fear, I have only love.
—FLEETWOOD MAC, "GYPSY"

♡

day 267

♥ : IF I HAD TO RANK SIGHT, SMELL, HEARING, AND VISION
IN ORDER OF IMPORTANCE, THE ORDER WOULD BE...

♥ :

day 268

...IS MY FAVORITE SENSE BECAUSE...

 :
_____

 ♥ :
_____

day **269**

IF I WERE A SUPERHERO, MY DOWNFALL WOULD BE...

♥ : _____

_____

_____

♥ : _____

_____

_____

day **270**

THE WORTHIEST OPPONENT OF ALL FICTIONAL VILLAINS IS...

♥ : _____

♥ : _____

YOU'RE **MY** SUPERHERO.

♡

day **271**

A BOOK I'VE READ LATELY AND LOVED IS...

♥ : _____

♥ : _____

day **272**

YOU SHOULD READ IT BECAUSE...

♥ : _____
_____
_____

♥ : _____
_____
_____

day 273

A WAY I LIKE TO TREAT MYSELF IS BY...

♥ : _____

_____

♥ : _____

_____

_____

day 274

THESE DAYS MY VICE IS...

♥ : _____

♥ : _____

When someone else's happiness is your happiness, that is love.

— LANA DEL REY

♡

day **275**

MY MOST DIFFICULT AGE WAS...

♥ : _____

_____

♥ : _____

_____

day **276**

BECAUSE...

♥ : _____

_____

♥ : _____

_____

day **277**

A LONG-TERM WISH I HAVE IS...

♥ : _____

_____

♥ : _____

_____

day **278**

A SHORT-TERM WISH I HAVE IS...

♥ : _____

_____

♥ : _____

_____

I don't have dreams. I have goals.

—GABRIEL MACHT AS HARVEY SPECTER, *SUITS*

♡

day 279

A LONG-TERM GOAL OF MINE IS...

♥ :
_____
_____

♥ :
_____
_____

day 280

A SHORT-TERM GOAL OF MINE IS...

♥ :
_____
_____

♥ :
_____
_____

day 281

A PLACE I'D LIKE US TO VISIT IN THE NEXT SIX MONTHS IS...

♥ : _____

_____

_____

♥ : _____

_____

_____

day 282

A PLACE I'D LIKE US TO VISIT IN THE NEXT SIX YEARS IS...

♥ : _____

♥ : _____

Traveling in the company of those we love is home in motion.

— LEIGH HUNT

♡

day **283**

IF I KNEW I HAD ONLY SIX MONTHS TO LIVE, I WOULD CHOOSE TO...

♥ :

♥ :

day **284**

IF I ONLY HAD SIX HOURS TO LIVE, I WOULD CHOOSE TO...

♥ :
_____

♥ :
_____

day 285

IF I CLOSE MY EYES AND GO TO MY HAPPY PLACE, IT LOOKS LIKE...

♥ :
_____

_____

_____

♥ :
_____

_____

_____

day 286

I THINK THIS IS MY HAPPY PLACE BECAUSE...

♥ :
_____

♥ :
_____

We loved with a love that was more than love.

—EDGAR ALLAN POE, "ANNABEL LEE"

♡

day **287**

THE MOST MEMORABLE MEAL I'VE EVER HAD WAS...

♥ : _____

♥ : _____

day **288**

THE MEAL WAS SPECTACULAR BECAUSE...

♥ : _____

_____

_____

♥ : _____

_____

_____

day **289**

YOU WERE RIGHT ABOUT...

♥ : _____

_____

_____

♥ : _____

_____

_____

day **290**

TRUE OR FALSE: IT'S HARD FOR ME TO ADMIT WHEN I'M WRONG.

♥ : _____

♥ : _____

Love is an act of endless forgiveness, a tender look which becomes a habit.

—PETER USTINOV

♡

day **291**

MY FAVORITE WAY TO UNWIND AFTER A LONG DAY IS...

♥ : _____

_____

_____

♥ : _____

_____

_____

day **292**

YOU CAN HELP COMFORT ME AFTER A LONG DAY BY...

♥ : _____

♥ : _____

day **293**

SINCE WE STARTED THIS JOURNAL, MY
PROUDEST ACCOMPLISHMENT HAS BEEN...

♥ :

♥ :

day **294**

SINCE WE STARTED THIS JOURNAL, WHAT I'M NOT SO PROUD OF IS...

♥ :
_____

♥ :
_____

Love is a door we shall
open together.

—CARL SANDBURG, "MOON RONDEAU"

♡

day **295**

A SHORT-TERM WISH I CAN MAKE HAPPEN FOR YOU IS...

♥: _____

_____

♥: _____

_____

day **296**

A LONG-TERM WISH I CAN MAKE HAPPEN FOR YOU IS...

♥: _____

_____

♥: _____

_____

day **297**

IF YOU WERE ANY ANIMAL, TO ME YOU'D BE...

♥ : _____

_____

♥ : _____

_____

day **298**

TODAY I AM THANKFUL FOR...

♥ : _____

♥ : _____

True love begins when nothing is looked for in return.

—ANTOINE DE SAINT-EXUPÉRY

♡

day **299**

MY FAVORITE NEW SONG IS...

♥ :

♥ :

day **300**

MY FAVORITE SONG OF ALL TIME IS...

♥ : _____

♥ : _____

day 301

IF YOU WERE A SONG, TO ME YOU'D BE...

♥ : _____

_____

_____

♥ : _____

_____

_____

day 302

I HOPE I AM YOUR...

♥ : _____

♥ : _____

day **303**

THE DUMBEST THING I'VE HEARD LATELY IS...

♥: _____

_____

♥: _____

_____

day **304**

THE SMARTEST THING I'VE HEARD LATELY IS...

♥: _____

_____

♥: _____

_____

day **305**

I'M GLAD ... HAPPENED.

♥:
_____

_____

♥:
_____

_____

day **306**

I'M SAD ... HAPPENED.

♥:
_____

_____

♥:
_____

_____

ANNA: "I LOVE YOU, MR. BATES. I KNOW IT'S NOT LADYLIKE TO
SAY IT, BUT I'M NOT A LADY AND I DON'T PRETEND TO BE."

BATES: "YOU ARE A LADY TO ME, AND I NEVER KNEW A FINER ONE."

—*DOWNTON ABBEY*

day 307

THE FIRST THINGS THAT COME TO MIND
WHEN I HEAR THE WORDS...

MAGIC: _____ _____

EAT: _____ _____

TANK: _____ _____

OWL: _____ _____

WATER: _____ _____

BLUE: _____ _____

day 308

IF WE WERE ON A REALITY SHOW TOGETHER, IT WOULD BE...

♥: _____

♥: _____

day 309

I WISH I WERE MORE...

♥ : _____

_____

♥ : _____

_____

day 310

I'M GLAD I'M NO LONGER...

♥ : _____

_____

♥ : _____

_____

day 311

I CONQUERED . . . THIS PAST YEAR

♥ : _____

_____

♥ : _____

_____

day 312

WE LEARNED TO . . . THIS PAST YEAR

♥ : _____

_____

♥ : _____

_____

day **313**

I'M STILL WORKING ON...

♥ : _____

_____

♥ : _____

_____

day **314**

WE'RE STILL WORKING ON...

♥ : _____

_____

♥ : _____

_____

Love is patient, love is kind.
IT DOES NOT ENVY, IT DOES NOT BOAST, IT IS NOT PROUD.
—CORINTHIANS 13:4

♡

day **315**

MY FAVORITE THING TO WEAR IS...

♥ :

♥ :

day **316**

IT MAKES ME FEEL...

♥ : _____

♥ : _____

day 317

IF I WON THE LOTTERY TOMORROW, I WOULD...

♥: _____

_____

_____

♥: _____

_____

_____

day 318

I WOULD NOT...

♥: _____

♥: _____

LIFE GIVES YOU LOTS OF CHANCES TO SCREW UP WHICH MEANS YOU HAVE JUST AS MANY CHANCES TO GET IT RIGHT.

—SARAH JESSICA PARKER AS CARRIE BRADSHAW, *SEX AND THE CITY*

♡

day **319**

MY GOALS FOR MYSELF FOR NEXT YEAR ARE...

♥ :
_____

_____

♥ :
_____

_____

day **320**

MY GOALS FOR US FOR NEXT YEAR ARE...

♥ :
_____

_____

♥ :
_____

_____

day 321

...IS NO LONGER IMPORTANT TO ME.

♥ : _____

_____

♥ : _____

_____

day 322

...IS MORE IMPORTANT THAN EVER.

♥ : _____

_____

♥ : _____

_____

PIGLET: "How do you spell 'love'?"

POOH: "You don't spell it...you feel it."

—A.A. MILNE

♡

day **323**

...DRIVES ME.

♥ :
_____

_____

♥ :
_____

_____

day **324**

...DRIVES ME INSANE.

♥ :
_____

_____

♥ :
_____

_____

day **325**

SPONTANEITY MAKES ME FEEL...

♥ : _____

_____

♥ : _____

_____

day **326**

PREDICTABILITY MAKES ME FEEL...

♥ : _____

♥ : _____

Love, work, and knowledge
ARE THE WELLSPRINGS OF OUR LIVES.
THEY SHOULD ALSO GOVERN IT.

—WILHELM REICH

♡

day 327

TRUE OR FALSE: I WOULD LIKE TO TRAVEL TO SPACE.

♥ : _____

♥ : _____

day 328

YOU SUPPORT OR REJECT MY DREAMS OF SPACE BECAUSE...

♥ : _____

_____

_____

♥ : _____

_____

_____

day **329**

THE BEST RELATIONSHIP ADVICE I'VE EVER GOTTEN WAS...

♥:
_____

_____

♥:
_____

_____

day **330**

FROM...

♥:
_____

♥:
_____

LOVE IS THAT CONDITION IN WHICH THE HAPPINESS OF ANOTHER PERSON IS ESSENTIAL TO YOUR OWN.

—ROBERT A. HEINLEIN, STRANGER IN A STRANGE LAND

♡

day **331**

A CLICHÉ THAT IS SO <u>TRUE</u> IS...

♥ :

♥ :

day **332**

A CLICHÉ THAT IS SO <u>UNTRUE</u> IS...

♥ : _____

♥ : _____

day 333

THIS NEXT HOLIDAY SEASON, I'M MOST EXCITED ABOUT...

♥ : _____

_____

_____

♥ : _____

_____

_____

day 334

THIS NEXT HOLIDAY SEASON, I'M LEAST EXCITED ABOUT...

♥ : _____

♥ : _____

NOBODY HAS EVER MEASURED, NOT EVEN POETS, how much the heart can hold.

—ZELDA FITZGERALD

♡

day **335**

...INSPIRES ME.

♥ : _____

_____

♥ : _____

_____

day **336**

IF I HAD ALL THE RESOURCES AT MY DISPOSAL, I WOULD CREATE...

♥ : _____

_____

♥ : _____

_____

day 337

THREE WAYS I'VE GROWN OVER THE LAST YEAR ARE...

♥ : _____

_____

♥ : _____

_____

day 338

THREE WAYS WE'VE GROWN OVER THE LAST YEAR ARE...

♥ : _____

_____

♥ : _____

_____

I WOULD RATHER SHARE ONE LIFETIME WITH YOU THAN FACE ALL THE AGES OF THIS WORLD ALONE.

— LIV TYLER AS ARWEN, THE LORD OF THE RINGS: THE FELLOWSHIP OF THE RING

day 339

A BAD HABIT I WANT TO BREAK IS...

♥ : _____

_____

♥ : _____

_____

day 340

A BAD HABIT I WISH WE COULD BREAK IS...

♥ : _____

_____

♥ : _____

_____

day **341**

ONE EVENT THAT HAS AFFECTED ME SINCE
WE STARTED THIS JOURNAL IS...

♥ : _____

_____

♥ : _____

_____

day **342**

THINKING BACK ABOUT THOSE MEMORIES, MAKES ME FEEL...

♥ : _____

_____

♥ : _____

_____

LOTS OF PEOPLE WANT TO RIDE WITH YOU IN THE LIMO,
BUT WHAT YOU WANT IS SOMEONE WHO WILL TAKE
THE BUS WITH YOU WHEN THE LIMO BREAKS DOWN.

—OPRAH WINFREY

♡

day **343**

MY WISH FOR THE WORLD IS...

♥ : _____

_____

_____

♥ : _____

_____

_____

day **344**

I'M CYNICAL ABOUT...

♥ : _____

♥ : _____

day 345

MY BUCKET LIST FOR THE NEXT YEAR IS...

♥ : _____

_____

_____

♥ : _____

_____

_____

day 346

ACTION STEPS I NEED TO TAKE TO MAKE THESE THINGS HAPPEN ARE...

♥ : _____

♥ : _____

Loving you is an adventure
I want to relive over and over.

♡

day **347**

IF I COULD SECRETLY GO INTO SOMEONE'S MIND AND CHANGE HOW THEY FEEL ABOUT SOMETHING, I WOULD CHOOSE...

 :

♥ :

day **348**

IF I COULD READ SOMEONE'S MIND, I WOULD CHOOSE...

 :

_____

 :

_____

day 349

MY BUCKET LIST FOR THE NEXT FIVE YEARS IS...

♥ : _____

_____

_____

♥ : _____

_____

_____

day 350

BUCKET LIST CONTINUED...

♥ : _____

♥ : _____

LIMITLESS UNDYING LOVE WHICH SHINES
AROUND ME LIKE A MILLION SUNS
IT CALLS ME ON AND ON ACROSS THE UNIVERSE.

—JOHN LENNON, "ACROSS THE UNIVERSE"

♡

day 351

THE BEST PURCHASE I'VE MADE LATELY IS...

♥ : _____

_____

♥ : _____

_____

day 352

I REGRET BUYING...

♥ : _____

_____

♥ : _____

_____

day 353

MY OUTLOOK ON . . . HAS CHANGED OVER THE PAST YEAR.

♥ : _____

_____

♥ : _____

_____

day 354

MY OUTLOOK ON THIS HAS CHANGED BECAUSE...

♥ : _____

_____

♥ : _____

_____

Love is the strongest force
THE WORLD POSSESSES AND YET IT IS
THE HUMBLEST IMAGINABLE.

—MAHATMA GANDHI

♡

day **355**

MY FAVORITE SNUGGLING POSITION IS...

♥ : _____

_____

_____

♥ : _____

_____

_____

day **356**

I THINK YOUR FAVORITE SNUGGLING POSITION IS...

♥ : _____

_____

_____

♥ : _____

_____

_____

day 357

NEXT YEAR I HOPE YOU HAVE...

♥ : _____

_____

♥ : _____

_____

day 358

NEXT YEAR I HOPE WE HAVE...

♥ : _____

_____

♥ : _____

_____

IF I HAD A FLOWER FOR EVERY TIME I THOUGHT OF YOU...I COULD WALK THROUGH MY GARDEN FOREVER.

—ALFRED, LORD TENNYSON

♡

day 359

THE LAST PHOTO I POSTED ONLINE IS...

♥ : _____

_____

_____

♥ : _____

_____

_____

day 360

I'D LIKE TO BE BEST REMEMBERED FOR...

♥ : _____

♥ : _____

day **361**

TO ME, OUR LOVE IS...

♥ :

♥ :

day **362**

MY BIGGEST HOPE IN LIFE IS...

♥ :

♥ :

LOVE IS FRIENDSHIP THAT HAS CAUGHT FIRE. IT IS QUIET
UNDERSTANDING, MUTUAL CONFIDENCE, SHARING AND FORGIVING.
IT IS LOYALTY THROUGH GOOD AND BAD TIMES. IT SETTLES FOR LESS
THAN PERFECTION AND MAKES ALLOWANCES FOR HUMAN WEAKNESSES.

—ANN LANDERS

♡

day **363**

MY WISH FOR YOU FOR THE NEXT YEAR IS...

♥ : _____

_____

_____

_____

_____

_____

♥ : _____

_____

_____

_____

_____

_____

day 364

MY WISH FOR MYSELF FOR THE NEXT YEAR IS...

♥ : _____

_____

_____

_____

_____

_____

♥ : _____

_____

_____

_____

_____

_____

"ANY DAY SPENT WITH YOU IS MY FAVORITE DAY. SO, TODAY IS MY NEW FAVORITE DAY."

—WINNIE THE POOH

♡

day **365**

HERE'S A DRAWING OF HOW I SEE YOU NOW.

♥ :